Guy de Maxence AFANDA

OVERKEYNES
ECONOMICS

+0 = -0

PART ONE:

The logueconomics
Or theoretical economics

INTRODUCTION

During its existence, the living being is subject to requirements. These needs, by nature, require him to seek satisfaction in telling him what to look for. To do this, he is forced to act in using the means available to him by constitution, namely his ability, or he is called to use instruments to be acquired, he must find out of him. Those instruments are the instruments acquired.

Now, access to the acquired instruments is essentially seeking, in that it is made against distances. So operations of access are simple acquisitions as capture or consumption, or more demanding acquisitions like sharing, prayer or production, they all prescribe a requirement, a path to cover, the path between the lack and satisfaction. The command is only prayer in the position of superiority; prayer is the command in the position of inferiority. These two behaviors are also demands.

As a result, we will have clear understanding of the particularity of the economy among multiple acquisitions. For this, the first act is to make an inventory of distances:

- interval
- incompatibility
- the absence
- latency
- impossibility
- the characteristic difference
- obsolescence.

Then, move or migration responds to the interval, the replacement responds to obsolescence, the choice responds to incompatibility, production responds to the absence, and increment responds to latency. The impossibility and the characteristic difference are irreducible.

In particular, the replacement must be seen as: processing, transfer, conversion and renovation. In growth, we must see: innovation, overinvestment, the capitalization and over-employment. In the movement, we must see: the service, the purchase, consumption, sale or makeup (balancing).

In economics, the royal road that gives us the opening expected is etymology. Indeed, the economy is oïkonomia (in Greek). Oïkos = home and nomia = organization. So: oïkonomia = home + organization. The economy is then the domestic organization, taken in relation to its size in the cradle. For replacing "home" to "community", the economy takes the magnitude of the overall organization. But a more relevant note says that the economy is more a relationship than a place characterized by a certain type of behavior that takes place there. In fact, organizing is to set roles and prerogatives. In a traditional sense, it is the share of labor and means acquired. In a word, it is to acquire by the distributive participation.

Indeed, consider a community that works as: $\Sigma T_i = +K$ (the sum of tasks performed as a capital acquisition) However, $+K = -(-K)$, where $-K$ indicates the deficit created in the source. Under the conditions of recurrences, the deficit must be offset in the form of compensation, or other income. In short, even at the

individual stage work hollow source, and determines the need for bailouts in terms of recurrences. For example, a well from which we draw water must remain useful by replacing the water drawn. It can acquire it in several possible ways. Likewise, the individual who is working vacuum energy to be recovered, in order to reproduce the same work after, or just to rehabilitate his energy. These observations confirm the following two findings:
1) the principle or law of acquisition: $+0 = -0$
 to acquire is to subtract, so: subtraction= acquisition
2) in the distributive participation, the law of the acquisition is both a collective and a individual concern. For the rest of the book, it will respond formally to the following questions:

. What is the economy?

. What are the forms of the economy?

. What are the magnitudes of the economy?
Logueconomics answers to the first question. The economomographics answers to the second question. Econometrics meets the third.

FIRST: The logueconomics

Logueconomics is the scientific discourse on the economy. Here indeed the economy is itself the object and the reference. Let us remember that the economy is the global organization, namely the group or community submitted to the division of labor and means acquired. In other words, the economy is a distributing participation. But let us also remember the law of the acquisition. This command first to distinguish: $acq(i, j, k, ...)$ and $(acqi, acqj, acqk ...)$, $acq(i + j + k + ...)$ and $acqi+acqj+acqk ...$

Then, the law prescribes to write that:

i acquiring= subtracting to i

(acqi= Subti)

or:

i acquiring= i subtracting to j.

But what does i loose for? Several scenarios are possible here. It is to answer this question economically. And economics, the law of the acquisition takes the form:

acquisition= contribution

or

$acqi = off\ i$.

Basically, you have to be careful here, noting that: acquisition = subtraction, or acq = subt, can be written as: 1) $acq°i = subt\ i\ to\ x$, or: $acqi= subt_i x$, so in the case of participation, we have:

$\Sigma acqi= \Sigma soust_i x$; but specifically here, which is the case of the federal participation (sum of several actions on a common subject): $\Sigma soust_i x= acq(i, j, k, ...)$, and therefore: $\Sigma acq\ i = acq(i, j, k, ...)$, or, $\Sigma acqi = acq(\Sigma i)$.

2) the necessary difference with distributive or economic interest is:

Sousti = offi= acq(i, j, k, ...), and therefore:

$$acqi=acq_i(i, j, k, ...).$$

In economics the law of the acquisition is:

Acqi=acq$_i$(i, j, k, ...), or:acqi = acq$_i$(i + j + ...). This writing schematically follows as: $\left[\sum [\text{acq i} = \text{acq}_i(i,j,k,...)] \right]_{\sum i}$, sufficient to show that: the economy is ordinary mutual acquisitions. Or, the exploitation or the creation of the "exchange = participation = distribution" as the mode of production and distribution of wealth. acq x + acqy = 0 , is the mathematical writing of exchange. And in common terms in economics, writing the widest is: acquisition+cost = 0.

For example, if we set @ for computer and $ for monetary sign, we have the following:

- 1 @ = $ -1000 (the cost of acquiring a computer here is $ 1,000)
- 3 candy = $ -75 (obtaining 03 candies cost $ 75).

In addition, in the mathematical writing of the economy, x and y may be communities or sets. Also, writing acq$_i$(i, j, k, ...), which means the public or universal offer of i (we read: acquisition of (i, j, k, ...) by i), writing math suggests the formula:

$$acq_i(i, j, k, ...) = (acq_i i = acq_i j = acq_i k = ...).$$

So anyway, the economy is fundamentally an exchange, under the aspect of the establishment of the exchange as a rule of organization. So here we have to write: exchange= participation. For acquisition, we must participate, be a contiguously transmitter and receiver element in the allocation process. Transmitter element is noted acq⁻ and the receiving element is noted acq⁺ˑ so good: acq⁺=acq⁻.

Writing mathematical economics still applies to the market, namely the reciprocal demand as shown here: request = exchange, features of the economy. Or take some examples:

- +07 rolls = -$800 (acqx = +07 rolls, acqy = +$ 800)
- -07breads = +$ 800
- -01coq = +10 mangoes
- +$16 = -4000 naira.

These examples clearly show what makes the difference in the economy relative to other modes of acquisition, because the economy is primarily an acquisition mode. A mode prescribed or suggested. The imperative or political economy is the economy: participation = distribution = exchange, or: acquisition=offer (for acquisition, must contribute, must offer). Here, economic processes and economic activities are determined in relation to community life. The equations relating thereto arising from the following fundamental and characteristic already noted:

$$\Sigma acq\ i = \Sigma acq_i(i,j,k,\ldots),\ \text{with card}(i,\ j,\ k,\ \ldots)= n,$$

where n is the size of the suppliying community. Before the next chapter let us notice again that in economics, acquisition = exchange, roughly. So is barter purchase or sale. What about the production, consumption and savings?

In an economic context, these are transactions related to trade, anyway. For example, a person wants to use (consume) his cell phone. He charges credit and electricity, means acquired in exchange for his case. Or, a craftsman who makes a pot, and to make use (consumption) of clay, scissors and others, practice exchange transactions in an economic context, where to get these materials and instruments, it must do so by purchasing barter or loan, which are versions of the application. So in a word, in economics, the acquisition is: $D = e$, where e is the exchange D the demand.

In addition, and overall the work is also an acquisition. Unlike here, the acquirer replaces the lack by creating, making, the course, the transformation or mutation. In an economic context, the work is an exchange or a medium of exchange. It can then exist as application or as a form of contribution.

In addition, the content of the work is a process that must be seen in the production as well as in consumption. The production is the creation or making. Consumption is the acquisition by transformation or mutation (e.g., credit put into the mobile phone is transferred by exchange the communication is established). In short, the formula of work is: $T = p + c$, or more precisely, $T = P + C$, we will specify more lately.

Finally, as to find out whether the balance is characteristic of the law of the acquisition in economics, just check the experience to compel relativism. Even in economy, the imbalance in the acquisition is possible. The egalitarian exchange is also likely that the unequal exchange. For example, a trader sets the worker that:

+1h = -$02, or: +$02 = -1hour. Or expertise indicates that: +1 roll =-30min = +$0.8.

In other words, the production time required or necessary to obtain a roll is 30 minutes. And this term corresponds to a gain of $ 0.8 for the employer. So, in an hour of work, while the worker earns $ 02, the employer earns $ 1.6. Thus, taken without any other consideration, there is imbalance in the exchange, and it is in favor of the worker.

SECOND: The economomographics

This part of the economic theory describes the structure of the economy.

The first case is microeconomy, the economy of economic sub-groups, that is to say subgroup where the exchange is ruling.

The second case is macroeconomy, the economy of the whole stage.

Then there is the intereconomy and political economy. Intereconomy is the market is or exchanges between macroeconomies. We readily agree that the federation of several macroeconomies is a larger macroeconomy.

Political economy is the economic organization operated by a public authority. It exists by the State by the mayor or by any political control whatsoever, as the establishment of the economy. Naturally, this establishment is the distribution and acquisition of wealth, which are activities necessary for the survival of the political and administrative order acquired. A territory inhabited by the shortage, rapine and raid, scatters. Culture, all achievements and alternate behaviors of a group exists if the source is localized, and this source is localized if it is the place where a macroeconomy unfolds. In short, political economy is the instrumentalization of microeconomy, macroeconomy and intereconomy to operate the acquisition and distribution of wealth.

In general terms, politics=economy+socionomy+culture. The new term here is socionomy. It is the set of characters or features that make the need of society, i.e.

all actions and acts that exist to create save and renew the social order. And since the social order is based on complementarity, actions and deeds in question are decisions of all kinds, necessary and conducive to the existence of this order. In terms consecrated the socionomy is all the decisions required by the company, that is to say the complementary relationship. These decisions are findings on the character of the social order, or regulatory acts such as law, the police or the Administration. The socionomy answers the question: how to live together in harmony? Because naturally, quarrels for the acquisition and possession of wealth, obstruct or endanger the harmonious social order, so necessary and useful to anyone eager to sustainable security. The exploitation of man by man, oppression, slavery and serfdom are indeed atrocious evidence that man is a complement of man.

- Production, we distinguish: the volume of production p, the variety of production (i.e. all families of production), digital production flow (the flow of the creation or formation of goods and services), the economic rate of production (the flow of production over expenditures or production costs), projections of production (the aspects of production in each family), counterparts and relative levels of production, and localized or compared frequency of the production. This range can be extended to other settings.
- The appetite is the flow of needs
- Overall demand is human operating ability (for shade, we can distinguish efficient demand)

within an economic framework. This capital consists mainly of individuals or groups of individuals seeking or supplying labor. The schematic writing of this statement is as follows:

offer of x = -acquisition for y
demand of x =-offer of y
but, acquisition of y = expenditure of y = -income for x
So:
$\begin{cases} offer = expense \\ acquisition = income \end{cases} = \begin{cases} Q = x \\ D = y \end{cases}$

and then: D+x= Q+y, the fundamental relationship of logueconomics.

It reinforces the idea that economic activity is an instrument for distributing wealth. The activity has somewhat the economic capacity of acquisition over the circulation of wealth in an economic framework. This ability is not only the income earned by contribution, you must associate it with the ability to work or the work force F_T, which then takes the position of potential income in the formula: PP = y + F_T + Z, where PP is the purchasing power or the economic ability to acquire, Z represents the marginal gains or acquired (or para-economic).

In macroeconomics, economic demand equation takes the form:
$\Sigma (Q + y)_i = \Sigma(D + x)_i$, with:
ΣQ_i = GDP (gross domestic product)
Σy_i = Ty (total income)
ΣD_i = GD (the general demand)
Σx_i = GC (general consumption)
It appears: GDP+Ty=GC+GD.
In intereconomics, with: ΣD_i = Y (imports), Σx_i = X (exports), we must modulate ΣQ_i and Σy_i, as follows:

13

$\Sigma Q_i = IPE$ (the inside product exported)
$\Sigma y_i = Yy$ (imported income);
and: $IPE + Yy = Y + X$.

* The market is the reciprocal demand. There are here two applicants face to face. Thus, x and y are in a market, if the following entry is admissible:
$D_x + D_y = 0$.
By extension, if there is market: $\Sigma D_i = 0$. It is the natural form of the market for D_i not zero. Now, the structural formula of the contract is: $Q_{\{i,j,k,...\}}$, where ijk... form the variety of the market. Also, card$\{i, j, k, ...\} = n$ is the n-offering market, so the market $Q_{\{i\}}$ is uni-offering. Any complex market is at least bi-offering, which is a multi-market. In fact, the market is complex; there are always at least two families of goods, unless the amount of money exchanged does not receive the status of a commodity.

* Money is primarily a number. Indeed, consider this case: a client comes to a vendor and asked him to perform rather work at the level of the extent of the amount of goods discounted, instead of money that he does not have. In case of agreement, it is necessary that the income can be monetary or not.
Two points follow from this:
1) the currency is used as a substitute for the last commodity
2) the money is held as hidden treasure in the offer;
In a word, money is also an asset. Its uniqueness is that it is a measure of labor in economics. Indeed, every framed thing is the result of a work, so simply a result, and hence

14

it is work ... done. So the money, even when taken as a political instrument of wealth distribution is at first an aspect of the work measurement.

Let us show it so simple and easy. Practice shows that: acquisition of goods+ amount of money = 0. But in the relationship:

+10 cocks = -1 goat, or you have to write that: amount of money = 0, or must write:

1 goat = quantity of money. However, one goat = amount of work, so:

Amount of work = quantity of money.

This relationship does not mean that work and money are of the same nature, it does mean that it is the work that determines the value of the currency. Thus, the proper standard for operating the flow of money is the standard work.

* Accounting is keeping operations and inventory in a document that mentions the gains, expenses, floats, dates (or even moments), places, brief transactions achieved delayed or expected, and stocks. For example, the acquired formula is: + a; borrowing is formulated: $\pm a$, it is a floating, floating input, the transfer is formulated:-a, loan or debt formula is: $\mp a$, it is a floating, a floating output, the project formula: …a; the canceled operation formula is Øa. Then we have a table:

+	-	±		...

A more elaborate table is as follows:

OPERATIONS				STOCKS		
+	-	±	dates	present	missing	states (1) ...

(1) stands for "amortization"
The parameters of adjustment or recovery essentially are: savings, investment, debt, import and export.
In turn:

 * Savings is the not used part of the income. May it be required?
Consider the economic agent whose income is y =+1000 and who acquires supplies with ∂ = -600, the reexpenditure. Savings of this individual is ε = 400.
Where the minimum formula: $y = \partial + \varepsilon$.
Suppose those supplies are: cabinet A for 150, food for 250 and rent L for 200. We have:

$$e = + A + L + food = -150-250-200$$

which provides the formula: $e = \varepsilon - y$ (which is also considered as a minimum formula under factors that can raise economic or not).
Naturally, in fact, the use of income is subject to more operations than the only expense. Each economic agent may hold a micro accounting, where are likely to appear receivables endowments repayments or even losses and investment.

16

* Investment is the formation of working stock. Working stock includes operators, posts (places of operations) and other consumables, which in economics should be treated as immanent positions (indeed, any consumable is a position, and any position is a consumable). For example, fuel, motor oil, the staff meals, electric current, are consumables (i.e. posts) that go unnoticed in some type of business but appear in accounting in the form of spending or operating expenses.

* Debt is debt demand, ie the demand for temporary relief (what debt is in economy, temporary relief). In economy, the debt doubles as an exchange; it is an exchange - to put it exactly -. The conclusion will return on it.

Here, the focus is on the ability to reduce the debt, the ARD. In short, the safety of debt is measured by its contribution as a service for the joined acquisition the increase in capital and solvency. Thus, if the debt operation is W, K the capital and σ solvency, debt is $|W|$ such that:

$$\Delta |W| = \Delta K + \sigma \Delta W.$$

In addition, the ARD = $(\sigma \Delta K, \Delta K > 0)$, or:

$$ARD = (\sigma \Delta K)_{\Delta K > 0}$$

THIRD: Econometrics

These are stocks, rhythm, variety and unevenness.
Various tables allow us to enter in the following outline
of this announcement.

1. Table of stocks

modes activities	operation	Stock	expense	
Production	P	P	P	$\hat{p}$
Consumption	C	C		
....				

2. Table of rhythms

rhythms objects	Digital Rhythm	Economic Rhythm	Relative Rhythm
Production	P_n 'or $_n$ p'	P 'or P'	(P ') or $_{...}$ (p') $_{...}$
....			

3. Table of asperities

Asperties objects	elasticity	level	frequency	quality	...
....					

4. Table of varieties

varieties events	VEGETABLES	Software	...
consumption			
....			

These tables show the two aspects of econometrics to consider: kineconometrics or kinetic econometrics on changes in inventories, and stateconometrics or statistic econometrics on the numbers of stocks. Naturally, the kinetic econometrics prevails in the density of operations. Just to expand it on the general fashion, let us build it on the variation ΔS of any stock S.

In practice, the change in the stock resulting in the sum of inputs Y_i added to the output X_j. In other words, $\Delta S = \Sigma X_j + \Sigma Y_i$. When operations are designed cumulatively, namely that to each Y_i even equal to zero is associated with one X_j even equal to zero, it is easy to obtain a series S_n such that:

$$\Delta S_n = \Sigma Y_i + \Sigma X_i.$$

The following table emerges the way to get S_n rigorously, while obtaining in the same way the digital pace of the activity, namely: $\partial S_n = S_n' \partial n$, where n is the order of operations combined. So:

n	Y_i	X_i	$(\Delta S)_i$	$\Delta_n S$
1	+10	-0	+10	+10
2	11	-21	-10	0
3	+04	-07	-03	-03
4	+40	-23	17	14
5	0	-20	-20	-06
...				

states: $\Delta S_n = \Sigma(\Delta S)_i$ .In addition, by analyzing ΔS_n, it is easy to obtain: $\Sigma \Delta S_i = \Sigma [|n+1-i| (\Delta S)_i]$.

This equation of series leads to:

$$\Sigma \Delta S_i = \Delta |\Sigma S_i| = |n+1| \Delta S_n - \Sigma i(\Delta S)_i$$

where n is the number of the input-output operations performed in connection with the cumulative analysis in the activity studied. We deduce:

$$\Delta S_n = \frac{\Delta |\Sigma S_i| + \Sigma i(\Delta S)_i}{n+1}$$

And with, $(\Delta S)_i = \Delta(S)_i$, we obtain:

$1°)$ $_n \Delta S_n = \sum(\Delta S)_i = \sum \Delta(S)_i = \Delta \sum(S)_i$

therefore:

$$S_n = \sum(S)_i$$

$2°)$ $\quad \Delta S_n = \dfrac{\Delta \mid \sum S_i \mid + \Delta \mid \sum i(S)_i \mid}{n+1}$

therefore

$$S_n = \sum_{i=1}^{n} \frac{S_i + i(S)_i}{n+1}$$

$3°)$ $\quad \sum S_i = \sum[\mid n+1-i \mid (S)_i]$.

To maintain the rigor of the analysis, it should be noted to remember that: $\sum \mid \Delta S_i \mid = \Delta \mid \sum S_i \mid$; and: $\sum i(\Delta S)_i = \Delta \mid \sum i(S)_i \mid$.

In addition, the basic element is the stock S, as taken at the start, and we can thus state the absolute stock: $S_a = S_m + S_k$, the sum of the changing stocks and static stocks. So: $S_a = \mid X \mid + \mid Y \mid + S_k$, the amount of output plus the amount of input, and static stocks.

Now, let us consider the economic pace. The basic fact is that in economy

$X_i = Y_i$, from: acquired=income, and, subtraction=output. It comes: $\alpha X - \beta Y = 0$, where α and β are the coefficients of conversion; further the relationship:

$\Sigma \alpha_i X_i - \Sigma \beta_i Y_i = 0$, leads to: $\Delta S_n = \Sigma \beta_i Y_i - \Sigma \alpha_i X_i$.

The relative pace is the digital rhythm of a stock compared to the digital rhythm of another stock, which is precisely the relative digital pace. For example, the digital pace of consumption according to output is: $\dfrac{c'_n}{p'_n}$. In a unified framework, it is $\dfrac{\partial c_n}{\partial p_n}$. There is also the relative economic pace. For example, with: $\begin{cases} \partial c_n = -\partial \hat{c}_n \\ \partial p_n = -\partial \hat{p}_n \end{cases}$, we get: $\dfrac{\partial c_n}{\partial p_n} = \dfrac{\partial \hat{c}_n}{\partial \hat{p}_n}$

The stock level noted h_S is the effective or accomplished measure S^+ of the stock relative to the necessary extent denoted $S^{\pm}$. This defines the level of an operation or activity (operation multiplied by the frequency). Note in addition, the available stock is S^+, S^* is the limit stock and the missing stock is S^- ($S^- = S^{\pm} - S^+$). So: $h_S = \dfrac{S^+}{S^{\pm}}$. For example, production is 100 @ (computers). This is actually available production, since the entire production is 150 @. This gives: $h_p = \dfrac{100}{150}$ 'so "two for three". In practice, this gives the following table:

Agents	a_1	a_2	a_3

Cases			
case1	2	0	0
case2	0	2	0
case3	0	0	2
case4	1	1	0
case5	1	0	1
case6	0	1	1

In each case, it emerges numbers featuring frequencies numbers, that is, the number of products obtained. The relative level of the stock either measured according to the measure of another stock (direct relative level), or it is its level with respect to another stock level (compared relative level). Thus, we have an economic agent, whose entry a day taken from others shows: $y^+ = 120$, $y^{\pm}=220$, $d^+ = 140$, $d^{\pm}=200$. The level of income that day is: $h_y=\frac{6}{11}$, that of the expenditure is: $h_d=\frac{7}{10}$. So: direct income level compared to spending that day is $(h_{y)d} = \frac{6}{7}$. And the level of income compared to the level of expenditure is: $h_{y/d} = \frac{60}{77}$.

FOURTH: Econometrics (continued)

This section is reserved for appetite. We write it A. It is the flow of needs. Noting the need β, then $A = \Sigma\beta_i$. As part of the continuous or serial process, appetite is formulated: $A_n = \Sigma (A)_j$, as conducive to its digital pace. Therefore, ΔA_n is ΔA placed or read in a cumulative process - as described in the previous chapter -.

That said, note that: $\Delta A = \Sigma\beta^+ - \Sigma\beta^-$, so the sum of the emerging needs less the sum of needs satiated. Moreover, experience suggests that the decline of the need matches with the consumption growth. In same, analysis provides it, under the appearance of a double regression: the regression of the need and the regression of an external stock. This stock is damped by a transfer process that takes the form of consumption here.

Suppose that the lack is the lack of 10kg of bananas. Or they must be produced, or they must be carried, or they are just to be eaten. If we produce, we must make efforts so spending calories, and even if there is use of machine or slaves, they must be supplied; consumption will necessarily occur. Whether to carry, it takes effort, and even if there is use of vehicle, beast or slaves, they still need feeding, consumption necessarily takes place.

These comments recommend that the consumption c is sated need, or when $c = \Sigma c_i$, the sum of the needs satiated, so $c = \beta^-$ or $c = \Sigma \beta^-_i$. Cumulatively: $_n = \Sigma (\beta^-)_i$. Consumption as operation, C, then the satisfaction appears as the process to satiate needs.

Now, for a providing overview of the theoretical shape of need, already note that:

need = capital - acquisition.

So:

$(Need)_0 = (capital)_0 - (acquisition)_0$

$(Need)_i = (capital)_i - (acquisition)_i$

therefore:

$\Delta(need) = \Delta(capital) - \Delta(acquisition)$.

But in economics, the acquisition is fundamentally demand, and demand is the exchange, hence:

$$\Delta\beta = \Delta K - \Delta E .$$

The comparative approach gives:

$$\frac{need}{condition} = \frac{condition - satisfaction}{condition}$$

Therefore, the needing (the level of need) and quality (the level of satisfaction), respectively h_β and q, related by the equation: $h_\beta + q = 1$. Hence: $q = -\ e^{\frac{\Delta\beta}{\pm}}$, where:

$e^\pm = \left| \ e \ \right|_{\beta=0}$ (the measurement of the acquisition at $\beta = 0$, so the necessary extent of the satiating acquisition).

Another writing of the quality is: $q = q = e^{\frac{\ddot{q}}{\pm}}$, where $\ddot{q}$ is the provision of a good or a service. So the quality is the level of contribution, and the contribution can be written as: $\ddot{q} = -\Delta\beta$. The utility takes its place here as the non-zero contribution. And taking the capital as a set of useful things, it should be measured as the sum of non-zero inputs, these inputs is active (or commonly used) or passive (or not currently used), used or reserved, and complete or incomplete.

In addition, the variety of appetite is all the needs felt by an individual, group of individuals or a system. Thus, an individual needs a computer, two candles, baskets of five and ten pairs of socks, mathematically, we have:

$A = \{K^\pm - @, K^\pm - 2b°, K^\pm - 5\Xi, K^\pm - 10ch\}. \ K^\pm = e + \beta.$

The propensity is also a relevant indicator of economic behavior. It is the highest frequency in a range of frequencies. Thus, compared to a β_i need the series of frequencies f_j related to the frequency of β_j is formulated: $f_{\beta_i} = \sum f_i$ the greater frequency indicates the propensity of the subject. For example, this baby for 10 feedings suckled three times background, incompletely twice, once he was content to hold the nipple in his mouth, and four times he has simply played. So the baby has the propensity to play.

In group economy - macroeconomy and political economy - the appetite is the magnitude derived from the number N of the community. Thus, we must distinguish between the different identifiable families of needs. There are the necessary common, recurrent or transient needs. They are the primary appetite. There are common optional requirements, recurrent or transient. These are the needs that the gratification is not necessary; they are below palatability.

Mathematically, this gives:

Stage	number	varity	writing
primary	N	N {A} $_i$	$A = N\Sigma\beta_i$
secondary	$m \leq N$	$\lvert m \leq N \rvert$ {A}$_i$	$A = \lvert m \leq N \rvert \Sigma\beta_i$

And in political economy, the relationship between appetite (especially primary) and supply (mostly primary too) is a priority. Referring to rough, it is particularly attractive to explore or observe the digital link between the two variables. The work may overcome the need? Does the need arises for necessarily to be appeased?

Take for illustration, the example of the environmental features. A more or less periods of recurring foods are produced by plants for example. Does the existence of these products create the need to eat, or rather, does it respond to needs that are likely to appear only these periods?

Still, the numerical ratio between supply and appetite, based on their respective digital rhythms remains - even for the theory - a concern that we solve as follows:

Need + acquisition = capital (present or absent).

FOR A CONCLUSION

The economy is a type of relationship based on an acquisition mode. The investigations carried out in the preceding pages, lead to confusion economy and distributive acquisition by trade. Participation and contribution just take direction - such as the distribution- of the exchange network, under the law of acquisition: $+0= -0$.

With the formula of economic demand:

$Q + y = e + x$, in which the group economy takes the form: $\Sigma Q_i + \Sigma y_i = \Sigma e_i + \Sigma x_i$, we have:

ΣQ_i = aggregate supply

Σy_i = distribution or overall distribution

Σe_i = aggregate demand

Σx_i = total expenditure

In short, wherever there is a mutual acquisition, there is a level of economy. It is easy to use the formula: subtraction = acquisition, to do so.

Indeed, when acquired, there is: $+ a = -b$, in all ways. Now, when it comes to introduce debt and aid in that context, you must write:

debt = subtraction, and:

aid = subtraction.

But the law of the acquisition has two aspects:

1) transfer: to acquire must be transferring, in which case,

acquiring for x = subtraction to y

2 °) the intertransfert: to acquire must be transfer in both directions, here:

Acquiring for x = subtraction to x .

Support by definition can not be economic. It is essentially a transfer. Debt, however, in an economic context, is possible. As follows:

debt of x = subtraction to x

equivalent to:

debt of x + acquisition of y = 0 , it must be that acq(y) takes the form of a guarantee given by x.

The economy is thus not a pure institution. It can be a manifestation of an instinct or a character who takes the institutional aspect according to an institutionnal way to keep it.

PART TWO:

The practical economics

or

the praxeconomics

INTRODUCTION

For good clarity, it is necessary to distinguish logueconomics and praxeconomics.

Recall that logueconomics is the scientific or the theoretical discourse on the economy. It seeks and says what the economy is into the economy itself taken as the reference. So it says the economy is the establishment of the acquisition by exchange, whether casual exchanges, or whether organic or distributive trade. It describes the different aspects of the economy, namely the micro, macro, and the inter one.

A deeper exploration in the economy leads to the sources the means the resources and the systems, and then we go full foot in the field of practical economics.

The source is the sum of the products. The means are operational or available gateways to the satisfaction or acquisition expected. Resources are the ability to redo; capacity or means to exhaust the source, or just to quench the necessary recurrence.

The praxeconomics is the discourse on the sources, the methods and the system in economy. In other words, the fundamental themes are production, the economic power of acquisition, the power of economic acquisition and the economic system. For about logueconomics, talk about source is talking about supply, whereas in praxeconomics, to talk of source is to speak of acquisition operation.

To go slowly, in logueconomics, production is essentially the existence of products or offer. In praxeconomics, production is the achievement equivalent to the fetch of products. For example, the inventor who devises his tool performs as fetching something (by his brain he is in a position of source).

In logueconomics, consumption is sated need, the acquisition by transformation by mutation or by translation. In praxeconomics, consumption is exhausting former production. In logueconomics, previews are sufficient instead of surveys, the overall premium on detail. In praxeconomics, concrete is the home of detail, and practice exercises on the details. In logueconomics, wealth is goods and services, or relevant acts and things (satiating acts or thing) acquirable by exchange. In praxeconomics, wealth is the work (the amount of useful work) and the performing works (the path of fruitful work). In other words, in praxeconomics, wealth is: outcomes and processes, operations, consumable operators and fruits. In logueconomics, the economy is decided; it is a decision, an institution. In praxeconomics the economy is an alternative.

FIRST: The production

We have in turn:

1. The source

The source is the sum of the products, s is the source and p_i any product, so: $s = \Sigma p_i$.

Basically, the source is the seat or place of an internal composition law (which for convenience we will refer to: characteristic internal link or own internal link, namely, for example, +, such as: $x_a + y_a = z_a$), which we denote here universally " @ ". As follows: $\Sigma p_i = p_1 @...@ p_n$

This link, in the case of storability, has the characteristic that for all p_i of s, $s @ p_i = p_i @ s = s$ and $s = s @ s$.

Conversely, any formation of deposit or storable stock leads to: s @ p_i = s. The composition operation is therefore not here unlimited addition, but a limted addition. This type of addition has a limitation in the appearance of complex immanent operations. Examples of limited addition are :

$$i@j = \frac{i+j}{1+ij/s^2} \quad ; \quad i@j = i+j-ij/s \quad ; \quad i@j = \frac{i+j-2ij/s}{1-ij/s^2}$$

Thus, the complement of each individual element is: $\varphi_i = \Sigma i - i = s - i$. In addition, when the composition operation is internal, that is to say, characterized by the presence of a universal element u, such that for every element of the group formed, $\varphi_{ui} = i$, ie the common complementary of i and u, the complementary of i and j is of the group:

$$\phi_{ij} = \Sigma i - \frac{\varphi_i \varphi_j}{\varphi_u}$$

By extension, $\qquad \phi_{ijk...} = \Sigma i - \dfrac{\varphi_i \varphi_j \varphi_{k...}}{[\varphi]^{n-1}}$.

2 - The mean

To get a result, to acquire in short, we must make a change. And the ability to produce change is just the mean here. So, to get a result R, the mathematical

formula used here is: $\Omega = \dfrac{\int_{S_0}^{S} \mu \partial x}{} = \dfrac{\int_{0}^{R} \mu \partial x}{}$,

where Ω is the operation, the mean μ and x is the ride of the mean.

When the work is done in several towed, the formula becomes: $\Omega = \sum \Omega_i$

Indeed, the notion of full extraction refers to a specific way. The full extraction indeed, is the amount of output per productive operation (that is to say, by operation necessary to obtain a complete product or fully concurrent stock of products). In other words, the full extraction is the volume of production achieved with an efficient operation. Thus, the difference between the labor or slow work and industry, the massive and rapid and steady work, is extra speed, precision and accuracy which can be translated to a simple multiplier. In this case, to make objects of a certain nature, a plant contains n people who make p similar objects simultaneously in a time t, the result is: np. Then one person makes mp at the same time and simultaneously with the other, the result is: mnp. The multiplier in question is (m - 1) n; it is the industrial multiplier. In cases where the bumps occur, m is replaced by $\sum m_i$.

This multiplier (generally so: $\sum m_i - n$) is an indication of increased resources. By asking: $mn = n^{\gamma+1}$, γ is the index of paratechnical power (supply from machines for example).

3 - The ressource

The resource is the ability to redo a necessary operation. It is somehow a return to the source. The usefulness of the source is to contain the product expected. Accordingly, we design the irreversibly exhaustible source or stiff source, the inexhaustible source and the resilient source.

The stiff source is the seat of an essentially unrenewable extraction. The extraction process here is conceivable in two ways:

- the sequential progression, whose expression is:

$$(\Delta s)_{i°} = k_i (\Delta s)_{i°-1°} \quad ; \text{ therefore with :}$$

$$(\Delta s)_{2°} = k_2 (\Delta s)_{1°}, \ (\Delta s)_{3°} = k_3 (\Delta s)_{2°} = k_3 k_2 (\Delta s)_{1°},$$

and then: $(\Delta s)_{n°} = (\Delta s)_{1°} \prod_{i=1}^{n} k_i$

$$\Sigma(\Delta s)_{i°} = (\Delta s)_{1°} \sum_{i=1}^{n} (\prod_{i=1}^{n} k_i)$$

$$\Sigma(\Delta s)_{i°} = - s_0$$

2) the cumulative growth, the expression of which is:

$$(\Delta s)_i = (1 + k_i)(\Delta s)_{i-1} \; ; \text{ hence, } \quad (\Delta s)_n = (\Delta s)_1 [\prod_{i=1}^{n}(1 + k_i)]$$

The spring source is finite but replenished temporally between two consecutive extractions.

1 °) in sequential write, the term base is:

$$(\Delta s)_{i°} = k_i (\Delta s)'_{i°-1}, \text{ with, } (\Delta s)'_{i°} = \rho_i (\Delta s)_{i°}, \text{ where } \rho_i$$

is the coefficient of stiffness less than 1 necessarily here .

$$\text{Accordingly, } (\Delta s)_{n°} = (\Delta s)_{1°} (\prod_{i=1}^{n} k_i \rho_{i-1})$$

- In cumulative writing, basic expression is:

$$(\Delta s)_i = (\Delta s)_{i-1} + k_i (\Delta s)'_{i-1} = (1 + k_i \rho_{i-1})(\Delta s)_{i-1} \; ; \text{ hence,}$$

$$(\Delta s)_n = (\Delta s)_i [\prod_{i=1}^{n}(1 + k_i \rho_{i-1})]$$

As for the inexhaustible source, $\rho = 0$ indefinitely. Also, with the relationship: $(\Delta s)_{i°} = k_i (\Delta s)'_{i°-1}$, here k is always infinite. And the direct relation between ρ and k, is given by the equation:

$$\Sigma(\Delta s)_{i°} = (\Delta s)_{1°} [\sum_{i=1}^{n} (\prod_{i=1}^{n} k_i \rho_{i-1})] \quad = - \frac{s_0}{n} \Sigma(1/\rho_{i-1}).$$

The exhaustion time of the source is $\dfrac{\sum (\Delta S)_{i^\circ}}{(\Delta S)_{1^\circ}}$ units of time requirement. This time is related to the frequency of need.

It leads back to the interest about the resource. It is required by the need return, and thus has the means frequency. Hence, to formalize the resource, it should be written: $\mu_\phi = \mu_{n^\circ} - \mu_{1^\circ}$, and:

$$\mu_{n^\circ} = \mu_{1^\circ} \dfrac{\sum (\Delta S)_{i^\circ}}{(\Delta S)_{1^\circ}}$$

Thus, it is better that the resource is the means by which the frequency of work is possible.

4 - Production

The production is the migration of wealth, from the source to outside the source, hence the:

$P = \Delta s = -p$, next, C, inherent consumption: $T = P + C$ (work) is: $C = \Delta K_T = -c$, where K_T is the working capital and c the volume of consumption. The practice shows that each time the work is both ebbs T^- and flows T^+, so: $T^\pm = T^+ + T^-$, like the practical writing of work.

5 - Investment

Since it is the formation of the stock of work or the capital of work, it has operators, consumables and economic features (or all economic means or all economic instruments: savings, loans, funds ...). This gives K_T the capital of work, such as: $K_T = \Sigma s_i + \Sigma \Omega_i + \Sigma c_{Ti} + \Sigma \&_i$; and therefore : $I = +K_T$.

For the clarity of the study, to distinguish for investment, and why not for the other variables, operational change $\Delta x = x_j - x_i$, and the statistical variation or stokometrical variation:

$\Delta_n x = x_{j^\circ} - x_{i^\circ}$. We must add the operostatistical variation: $\Delta_\omega x = (\Delta; \Delta_n) x = (x_{k^\circ})_j - (x_{k^\circ})_i$; and the stokooperational variation :

$$\Delta_s x = (\Delta_n; \Delta) x = (x_k)_{j^\circ} - (x_k)_{i^\circ} \ .$$

At the end, each case brings into a particular analysis, operational analysis, stokometrical analysis, operostatistical analysis or stokooperational analysis. There is perconstance or stationary if: $\Delta_n x = 0$, $\Delta_\omega x = 0$ or $\Delta_s x = 0$.

SECONDLY: The economic power of acquisition

Power is the presence of the capacity. In economics, it is the presence of the exchange capacity. It is the purchasing power, the possibility of obtaining by exchange. Here, the exchange is inquisitive, it is the quest for product in replacement of a part of the capital held, it is buying. Today, with money, it is easier to define the purchase as obtaining a product in exchange for a monetary amount.

For the study, let K_e be the exchange capital. The purchasing power is $\pi = K_e / \sum \beta$, so capital K_e took over the costs of the needs. But economically, $\sum \beta = -x_n$, where x_n is the expenditure required.

So: $\pi = - K_e / x_n$, is the countable purchasing power. For the real exchange capital from the market is:

$$\pi K_e = - K_e^2 / x_n$$, which is the purchasing power compared.

For accuracy, $K_e = m^+ + m^-$, ie the sum of goods (m^+) and equivalent or substituent (m^-) of goods. Indeed, the goods is the thing sought or offered in exchange for an equivalent or a substituent. Finances are part of the capital, and are the multiplicand capital of exchange, namely the offer made for its growth (eg, the money used to get more money). The charges are the dividend capital

41

of exchange, namely the capital to spend or the money amount that decreases by exchange.

In the case of finance, mathematical writing is:

$$-x_i = +x_j = +x_i + kx_i + q \; ; k = \hat{\imath},$$ is the interest rate, q is the total emission flux.

THIRD: The power of economic acquisition

Economic power of acquisition concerns demand, as the ability to obtain satisfaction offering the substituent. The satiating object meets a specific need, while the substituent only complies with the law of economy: for getting, participate or offer something in return.

In contrast, the power of economic acquisition is the ability if not the opportunity to participate in an economic system, as the capacity or ability to provide the satiating object getting the substituent.

For example, is in the position of economic power of acquisition, the individual who wants a drug m and offers a jewel b taking to the holder of drug who does not want b, but takes it with respect to its exchange value.

Is in position of power of economic acquisition, the individual who has a goat for his contribution to economic participation, or as the cost for a substituent.

There is the case where a satiating object is exchanged for another satiating thing, so the economic interpower of acquisition. If a substituent is exchanged for a substituent, is interpower of economic acquisition.

That said, it must be remembered that in logueconomics, market is reciprocal demand. But in praxeconomics, we must describe the process.

In praxeconomics, the market is: $(+ x = - y)_{D1} = (-x = +y)_{D2}$

In praxeconomics,

1) for the purchase, we have: $(-y...+x)_D = (+y...-x)_Q$

2) for sale, we have: $(+x...-y)_D = (-x...+y)_Q$.

For explanation, writing (a ... b) reads "a precedes b" or "b follows a". Hence, for the purchase, demand precedes the offer, and for the sale, supply precedes demand.

A case of the power of economic earning, that is to say, the power to sell, is the enterprise. Indeed, business, in economy, is the service done by production of services, by provision of services or by manufacturing goods operators. At this level, we must distinguish the goods operators (machinery, equipment, ...), economic goods (money, the ability to work, substitutuent, pledge), consumables and capital goods shelter (drinking glass, clothes, ...).

After that, the power to sell, in turn, is linked to the quality of K_e. It is in fact the quality of K_e, taken independently of the market. Taken according to the market, it is also linked to the purchasing power of the customers, hence the relation: $y_{a/b} = \pi_b(q_a(K_e))_b$

44

In other words, the power of sale of a over b is strictly related to the purchasing power of b and to the quality of the capital of exchange of a at b. Or the power of sale is the exchange capital taken in relation to price.

The attractivity, that is to say the easiness to sale, follows the same relativity. Already, it requires the value of K_e. But the value of a thing z is: $v(z) = -\Delta\beta$. Also, $v(K_e) = -\Delta(\sum\beta_i)$. Now, $\sum\beta_i = x_n$, then : $v(K_e) = -\Delta x_n$.

Also, before we go any further, the analysis recommends distinguish $K_{e+} = m^-$ the capital purchase, and $K_{e-} = m^+$ (merchandises), the capital of sale.

FOURTH: The economic system

How to make economy? Thus formulated, the question receives the response, it is sufficient to establish a permanent distributive participation.

By definition, participation is a group operating. In other words, each element i of the group performs concurrent operation ω_i, such that: $\Sigma\omega_i = \omega_{\Sigma i}$. It appears immediately that: $\omega_i = 0$, gives that: $i = 0$, or that i is standing by. When there is distribution, $y_{\Sigma i} = \Sigma y_i$.

Then there is how to make the economy. In other words, how to access or make access to the distribution of wealth?

Is it by rent, contract or membership?

Briefly, note that the rent is paying for use. Here, the offeror of income is the borrower.

The contract is an agreement between:

      i.   two suppliers of labor and therefore two job applicants

ii.   a job applicant and an offeror of work, and therefore an income demander and an income offerer
iii.   two income demanders .

Membership is actually constitutivity. Namely, that the bond of community (co-presence) and more the link of community (coparticularity) and even the link of company (or complemetarity), are the principles of the participation required. Thus, the co-belonging to a country or coconstitutivity to a country is an incentive principle of participation.

This incentivity is particularly intractable that it is driven by the need for independent living. In other words, in political economy, each individual capable of independent living is required to participate in community living by a lucrative daily activity and of general utility.

Hence, the existence and circulation therefore the distribution of wealth is held or conducted by the efficient demand volume, money and prices.

1) The efficient demand is the sold offer in logueconomics; better, the contract is reciprocal acquisition where the work and the amount of work are goods for sale. In praxeconomics, it is the extraction or the formation of wealth; in political economy, it is the exercise of a profession. Specifically then, the contract, the work, is the exercise of the labor force or the deployment of the economic capacity of acquisition. In

other words, if F_T is the labor force or the ability to work, the work is its course, so:

$T = \int F_T \, \partial s$. This is the work for sale in economy, not F_T .

2) The positive rate of a work, then the cost of compliance with the requirement, namely here, the amount of work required to produce, or to obtain the desired result. Thus, the cost of labor is: $-T = p + c$, the positive cost; it is physical.

In capitalism, the work is written: $\vec{T}_i^{\,j} = P_i + C_{i,j} = - p_j - c_i$, i works for j, where: $y_i = \hat{P}_j - \hat{C}_i$, is the income of i, as the combined consumption $C_{i,j}$ is attributed to i.

The optional price is related to the mobility of the quality of the product, or to the purchasing power. In fact, the price related to the mobility of quality is more specifically the gradient price. If q_p is the product quality, the gradient price is $q_p \hat{p}$. The optional or speculative price suggested by the attractiveness of the product, namely the judgment which increases or underestimates the value of the product, since the attractiveness of a product is the density of demand around it. The speculative price is then $v_a(p)$, the value of the product according to the judgment of a. with Ψ_a the coefficient of speculation, the price is: $\psi_a v(p)$. If in addition the quality of the product or wealth varies, the speculative price takes the form: $v_a(pq_p) = \psi_{aq} v(pq_p)$.

3) Money is the number given equivalent to the goods. Known as the general equivalent of commodities, it is

called something which equivalence with the goods is established by definition or decision. One would like to retain the sense that money is more support or place of the amount written or monetary value. But declare 10yens, not revisit conceptually support, but rather a quantity or an equivalent degree. Indeed, if the positive price of a product is converted into money market rate, it appears that this amount of money is an alternative equivalent amount of work.

In fact, any merchandise is - or at least has - the amount of work. Thus, if the positive price is p, and the monetary price p_m, l is the link of equivalence as: $p_m = lp$. But money is a container. And it is even more recipient it offers goods, that is to say, the quantities of labor. Better yet, it can be offering work against exchange of goods. Suppose, for example, establish that in return for work goods are obtained, it would break immediately sluggish sales for example. The idea here is that $l = 1$. For work exchanged plays the same role as the currency, but it offers a particular goods or goods singled by a particular content. Money offers an indistinct promise of goods. Its value is the equivalent of all the work; it is the universal equivalent of labor.

Indeed, as work, money is an amount of work, and here money = goods. But as a yardstick, a quantity of money is a quantity of goods. The absorbency of the currency is then $å = l^{-1}$. But any amount of quantity is a quantity, and this: money = work, and for economics, work = good. Hence, working with: money = work, we have: $p_m = p$, and so: $l = å = 1$. Specifically, all work is then measured in pulses, ie, in complete minimal amounts of work required. If σ is a pulse, $p = n\sigma$, or $p = \Sigma\sigma_i$. But for continuity, writing $p = n\sigma$, gives n the frequency of σ.

Finally, work = money, offers: effective work = available currency. Effective work is work done or available, so the potential work leaves:

potential work = potential money = workforce.

FIFTH : The practical accounting

It occurs in three previous steps. First, the level of positions, then the level of stocks and finally the level of mobility of stocks.

1) The level of positions

Positions				Stocks	
rank	Date	place	schedule	name	amount

2) The level of stocks

Stocks		Properties			
name	amount	rank	source	Nature	category

3) The level of mobility of stocks

Stocks		Operations			
name	rank	Nature	cate gory	agent	goal

The prologue of this accounting is the balance sheet as follows:

REVIEW						
stage	date	schedule	modification	place	exchange	place

For example, consider the case of a transfer of 60 13kg bags of rice.

1) The levels of positions

. rank: 03

. Date: 10/06/2010

. location: shop

. time: 10:20

. Designation: bags

. quantity: 60

2) The level of stocks

. Designation: bags

. quantity: 60

. rank: 03

. source: Ets X

. nature rice

. category: 13kg / u

3) The level of mobility of stocks

- ...

- ...

. type: exit

. credit

. Agent: Chief Storekeeper

. goal: delivery

4) The balance sheet

. Step: 4

. Date: 10/06/2010

. time: 10:20

. Modified: -60sacs= -60 × 13kg rice

. location: shop

. return: debt certificate

. place: cash.

SIXTH: The economic balance

In logueconomics, the economic balance is equal:

$$D + x = Q + y.$$

In praxeconomics, balance is: $I + x = P + y$; but:

$P = T - C$, so: $I + x + C = T + y$, and:

$\Gamma + I = T + y$, where Γ is the sum of the charges.

But political economy requires both combine all that and refer to mathematical statistics. It looks just like this:

1) a sample or a population is a set, then a cluster of identical or equivalent things from a common distinctive or discriminating feature, this discriminator is the community link or a mode or a character or another. In Math we have things x_i sharing the common discriminator δ, $\{x_1, x_2, ..., x_n\} = n\delta$, n is the number of δ, and we denote $\delta^{(n)}$ to indicate δ and its number. When a sample

is varied, that is consisted of classes or subsets defined by internal common discriminators δ_i, it is written:

$\{x_1, x_2, ..., x_n\} = n\delta = n_1 \delta_1 + n_2 \delta_2 + ... + n_p \delta_p$, with: $n_1 + n_2 + ... + n_p = n$. Each class is recorded: $\delta_j^{(nj)}$. The sample is multimodal if we write:

$$\{x_1, x_2, ..., x_n\} = (n\delta_1, n\delta_2, ..., n\delta_n).$$

2) We are in the case of a unimodal population. The universal modality is δ. Its number is n. Here we have a series or clusters ijk…, the median center c such that:

$\Sigma (c - i) = 0$. The development gives $c = \dfrac{\Sigma i}{n}$. When there is repetition and therefore frequency, the writing is: $c = \dfrac{\Sigma f_i i}{\Sigma f_i}$, which is the median, the arithmetic mean.

The cluster is continuous if it contains c, so the series. When each part of the clusters is assigned a coefficient γ, the centroid or effective center g such that:

$\Sigma\gamma_i (g - i) = 0$, so $g = \dfrac{\Sigma \gamma_i i}{\Sigma \gamma_i}$. The series is dispersed if g is at the exterior and concentrated if g is inner, so the cluster.

If the median and the centroid (or weighted average) are separate and constituent, there is tropism, if they are distinct and non-constituent, there is divergence, if one is constitutive and the other not, there is convexity if g is not constitutive and concave if g is constitutive, if the two are combined and component, there is equivalency, if the two are confused and not constitutive, there is convergence.

Now, the coefficient of g makes the equation:

$$\Sigma i(\gamma_g - \gamma_i) = 0, \text{ where:}$$

$$\gamma_g = \frac{\sum i\gamma_i}{\sum \gamma_i} \;.$$

In the specific case of a statistical population, the middle

$$\delta_c^{(n_c)} = \frac{\sum f_i \delta_i^{(n_i)}}{\sum f_i}$$

class is: ,and : $\delta_g^{(n_g)} = \dfrac{\sum n_i \delta_i^{(n_i)}}{\sum n_i}$ is the modal area of equal weighting, it divides the series or the cluster into two sub-modal areas that appear as a tropism showing surplus, deficit or equal aspect, provided that the average is taken for the center of weighted benchmark. If necessary for accurate detailed designate the weighted average as the discriminating threshold, it must also be designated as the center of the discriminatory mark.

Therefore, for analytical purposes, we must distinguish the below difference of the modality ε_m as: $\delta_m \leq \varepsilon_m \leq \delta_g$, where δ_m is the lower class, and the above gap of the modality ε_M such that: $\delta_g < \varepsilon_M \leq \delta_s$, where δ_s is the upper class, so that any displacement of the discriminating threshold is performed according to the ride Δh of the estimated rate of relevance:

$$h = -\frac{\varepsilon_m}{\varepsilon_M} + \frac{\varepsilon_M}{\varepsilon_m} = \frac{card\varepsilon_M}{card\varepsilon_m} - \frac{card\varepsilon_m}{card\varepsilon_M}$$, the position indicator of tropism.

Staff mobility rests on the basis that: $n_\varepsilon = \sum (n_i \in \varepsilon)$.

3) We are now in the case of a multimodal population. Here, there is complexity of the statistical description. The combined description achieves modal complex $(\delta_i , \delta_j , ...)$ as its base. As a result, the multimodal median is: $(\delta_i , \delta_j , ...)_c = (\delta_{ic} , \delta_{jc}, ...)$, and the threshold of discrimination is : $(\delta_i , \delta_j , ...)_g = (\delta_{ig} , \delta_{jg} , ...)$.

Any comparison operation in this statistical case, like any other kind of relevant operation, is more complex than the same operation in the case of a unimodal population.

For political economy, multimodality of the statistical population is the relevant case. For the investigation on the equilibrium, it is efficient to use the modal dichotomy, which is a method to couple a modality with its counterpart; for example, the production and income. There is equilibrium if the relevant indices are equal, so if: $h = h'$.

Again, the concept of system is suitable for the essence of the economy, namely the issuer is necessarily receiver too. The equation: $+a_i = -\hat{a}_i$, expresses it quite clearly. Therefore, in an economic unit producing with n agents, the appearance of circuit appears within that single remark that the circuit being closed path or paths, where the agent is receiver namely sender and recipient, there is numerical or quantitative equilibrium if all agents are also receivers, and if all receivers are also agents, and there is qualitative balance if each contribution is equal to the received, and each received is equal to the contribution.

Mathematically, the first case reads:

$\Sigma T_i = \Sigma acqi$, so T for work. The latter reads: $\Sigma P_i = \Sigma acqi$, so P for production. Any other writing indicates the imbalance. In other words, the economic balance remains supply branch equal to demand branch.

But against goodwill, this balance may be inaccessible due to unfavorable economic and living conditions; against goodwill, because conjuncture is greater than the agents that behave like the awaiting elements of its structure. Indeed, this situation is the combination of necessary attendances. But something is necessary if its absence is impossible. Mathematically, we have:

$[(i \neq k) + (j \neq k)] = k$, i and j are necessary with respect to k.

In the case of the necessary conditions, factors or agents or causes and necessarily related elements, are united so that the general fate gives itself as an equation to be solved within the limits it sets. It answers the questions: what is it? What should be? What is missing? What to do? How? Why? Who or what to do it? Against what? Where? When?

FINAL PERORATION

Moments like high cost of living and the economic crisis, challenge eminently State indeed. Through its duty of justice constituent of its value and foundation of its value, the State as public authority is first supposed to react and act to counter the likely individualists. In fact, keep the organic state as the economic short-circuit tends to boost demand in confusion or competition, is in the sovereign guarantee to respond by boosting or macroeconomic adjustment. It is to answer to a broken circuit:

Production ... exchange ... income, income... exchange ... (consumption, investment, ...); or rather answer to the break of balance.

Yes, sometimes the main situation stands in sharp obstacle such as a climate annoyance that causes a decline in production, which in practice leads to inflation, because of the opportunity offered by the superiority of demand over supply. But in economics, demand is the exchange. So the supply-demand imbalance is a crisis, especially if the supply is less, since in economy offer is to acquire, and ask it is proposing to offer, so it is acquiring.

The State therefore, as the sovereign grant of the global organic state, should primarily or completely or restart the sequence: request ... offer ... acquisition, restoring otherwise by introducing Keynesian full employment, or today's total trade (in the sense that economically, being present is being exchanging), or adjust the chain ensuring fairness if not the conductance of fixed prices. Indeed, in the chains: demand ... price fixed ... acquisition, and: offer... fixed prices ... acquisition, there is conductance of fixed prices if q_y is the quality of the income (or even more for the capital of the exchange K_e) so that:

$$q_y = \frac{y}{x_n}$$, q_y is y compared to a sample of selected needs.

It follows indeed that the economic crisis is a sign of a shortage, the supply in this case. Costly life still is regression index, but the blocking stop of the offer is deeply uneconomic, it breaks the acquisition by exchange, and dissipates macroeconomics. The financial crisis is distinct from the economic crisis only when money replaces the work. Even in a difficult and strong conjuncture which strongly blocks the effective response against the shortage, we must give as necessary, the welfare of work. Suppose the case of a severe and prolonged drought. In reality, it makes necessary a greater force of work to transfer water and operate irrigation.

As it appears, the economic crisis can still be attributed to external hostile forces. But costly life gives to suspect internal deviance of the economic network. As soon as the single monetary liquid determines or establishes the ability to acquire in the economic system, then the money priority is a law. This results in the unreliability of money (currency) compared to its unique value. Speculation indeed is established by distinguishing the fixed cost and the positive cost.

The fixed cost is introduced and implemented according to options. The price set is optional, and the price set is arbitrary if speculative. The positive cost is the amount of labor required to produce a product or perform a service, it is the labor cost and it is independent of the option, it is demanding. Costly life reports both speculation and recession as adversities in economics (and certainly macroeconomics), as the priority of money is the law. For the market, there has: manufactured goods (made by man), millers goods (made by machines), the eco goods (made by the flora, fauna, insects and microbes) mineral goods (provided by soils), which reflect the manufacturing and other works, such as suppliers of relevance to the equation: merchandise = amount of work.

It recalls that work is the process of making wealth (goods and services). Accordingly, we must leave the priority of the money to enter the priority of work, according to which, it is the amount of work that determines the volume or money to deploy, this volume of work is the work done or to be done.

The State must establish otherwise maintain economicalism or economism, namely the duty by law to participate lucratively in the global economic system, for any healthy person in legal age to pursue a career (because economism is all related to the formal insertion of all human labor or demand in the economic system), every human being is a material formula of the work force. It is a break with capitalism; exceed this economy of the couple boss-employee, which excludes from social well-being and good purchasing power, one who is neither owner nor employee. In fact, capitalism is underemployment, if we talk about employment rather than demand because it is the exclusion of some available workers off the cycle of the official economy.

It is performism that offers redemption; it is the implementation of worker's capital as prior; concretely:

1) the worker's capital (capacity or labor force, and work) is a prerequisite to financial capital

2) the contract is the boss, in economy and for economics, there is only applicants, and each applicant is an offeror

3) the ability to work is a form or a state of the currency, which is the potential currency or energy currency; Karl Marx wondered what the boss pays to the employee: work or the work force? We answer him easily the boss pays the employee's work, since the salary the employee receives is nothing other than the conversion of its ability to work in liquid currency. In a word, every work has its monetary equivalent, and also work is got with exchange of labor.

The economy is feeding lining for politics. Originally indeed, the economy is the global organization based primarily on the division of labor and income. The economy is primarily an acquisition mode, a distributive acquisition mode. This explains that the policy which the substrate is the collective life, as far as the economy, can only have its sustainability upon the prior comfort of the members of the community.

Here, political economy is the requirement that receives the policy; keep the economy as an instrument of social cohesion and stability. It has the essential care to answer the question: how to survive together without parasitism against each other? Policy in his case is responsible for responding to the question on what everyone wants; that is to say, how to live together without abuse against each other? This task is thus incompatible with the market economy.

The market economy excludes or denies the social base, it is not appropriate for politics and the economy.... It is the partial economy, since the market is one of the constituent elements of the economy. In the economy, in fact, there is the company, the market and the contract or institution (tenure).

Hence primitive economy is characterized by:

1) the collective land ownership

2) the consensual distribution of production

3) the commensally participation in production.

Because of its incompatibility with the individual expansion, it is outdated and replaced by the feudal economy, which characters are:

1) the private ownership of land

2) the rent due to the landowner

3) the duty prescribed to the other occupants of the earth subservient, to rent.

In turn, because of its incompatibility with the bourgeoisie lifestyle based on wealth acquired and maintained by the client demand for labor, the feudal economy is then itself obsolete and replaced by the capitalist economy characterized by:

1) private ownership of production equipment of the needer of work

2) the patronage of the needer of work and the proletariat of the offeror of work

3) grabbing profit by the work buyer.

Today, because of its incompatibility with the absence of unemployment, it must be overcome and replaced. Indeed, the principle of unemployment in capitalist economy, where labor is the subordinate service to a work client, provider of livelihoods.

In fact, capitalism has two highly challengeable characters:

1) the employer-employee pair

2) the exclusion of part of the productive humanity from the formal distribution of wealth.

The turpitude of the first character is as follows:

boss = requester of the service = payor

employee = offeror of the service = requester of pay;

so that in a relation between two demanders, one has the authority and the privilege for advantage. But in economy, there is no boss or employee, there are only demanders.

The turpitude of the second character is to put the cart before the horse, putting finance before work. But take 10000euros liquid, and ask them to build us an avenue. We do not get anything. But ask the people to build us an avenue with 10000euros, we shall find people who can do it. In the under-development, lack of schools and their equipment, so lack of human labor. There is a lack of health centers, hospitals and missing their equipment, it lacks the permanent availability of drinking water and the current domestic energy, so basically it lacks the human labor. There is a lack of roads, urban roads, complete telecommunication networks, social centers for special education children, women and the disabled, so it lacks the human performance. Along with the rest of the world, we must curb multiple crises (food, financial, humanitarian, health, diplomatic, security, climate, economic, social, political, identity, techno, and even anthropological and ethical), now more than ever it calls for human labor.

Thus, performism resets the source of the work (Man, for example) upstream of wealth. Wealth is not plenty of money, and poverty is not lack of money, but rather now, wealth is the performance capacity, and poverty is the inability of performance. Here, the boss is the contract. We must get out of the money as the prior to entering the ability to perform as the prior, which is to bring the money according to the amount of work available. Moreover, the food crisis is quite eloquent on the inability of the currency, as flourishing as it is, to replace the food or food production.

Man = to need (obligation of pittance), Man = group, Man = factory (source of wealth), and it is an inalienable right or obligation on positive political economy (as respects the inalienable essence of things) pose as a prerequisite for efficiency and strength that man is the pre-requisite wealth for wealth growth.

To finally end, a contribution due to perfomism is the elimination of speculation in economy. Already, speculation is the discourse on the probability. In practice, it is the mediation of probabilities, and more specifically in economics, it is the market of probabilities or worse the regime of random capital (or possessions).

In economy precisely, evil is that the flow of probabilities doubles as a real cash flow or a reduction in real stock; for example, against the likelihood of an increase in value (the value of a share hold, for example), some are actually spending their savings; but the success of the operation or the validity of the risk remains uncertain. More extended, speculation (in economy in effect) is the acquisition or purchase probability in a market of probabilities (the financial market, mortgage or borrowing).

The financial crisis in addition to the economic crisis (which is both cause and effect of the now shameful unemployment rate), is the revelation about the harmfulness of speculation in economy. When a customer purchases goods or securities in the only hope to sell more expensive, what does he do, if not he bought the likelihood? When a client usurer mortgages his palace for a loan with a financial value lower than the financial value of the palace, in the draft to get more money than borrowed, what is it, if not he has acquired probability? When a bank customer obtains a loan without pledging at the bank, which simply provides a referral to insolvency, what is it, if not he has acquired probability? When a bank makes loans with savings accounts of its payable clients, then replacing cash by promises of repayment, what does it do, if not it replaces the actual liquidity by probabilities.

www.ingramcontent.com/pod-product-compliance
Lightning Source LLC
Chambersburg PA
CBHW051818170526
45167CB00005B/2065